More Seeing is Believing

by Derek Belsey

The scene pictured above is a complete escape from the hectic, noisy and sometimes stressful life that most of us lead and I hope it will encourage more of you to go out and share the wonders of nature while they still exist.

Dedication

I dedicate this book to my very understanding wife - Patricia.

Contents

All photographs are by the author with the exception of some by Cliff Reddick.

ISBN 0 9530734 1 6

Published by Derek Belsey
Tel: 01932 241886

Designed by Robert Antell-Abbey Graphics.
Printed by Ian Allan Printing Ltd.

Introduction

Because my first book, *Seeing is Believing*, was quite successful I have been urged by friends and other people, some of whom I have never met, to produce another. As anyone who read the first book will have realised, putting pen to paper and producing a professional manuscript is not something that comes particularly easy to me so being urged to produce a second book, while no doubt very flattering, also presented me with something of a problem. Nevertheless, I decided to try again. There were several reasons for being persistent, not least of which was the satisfaction of breaking-even with my first foray into the complex world of self-publishing – a measure of success and acceptance which had been beyond my wildest dreams. More importantly and even more rewarding was the sheer volume of favourable comment and friendly correspondence which reached me from all parts of Britain.

One such letter came from a reader called Brian Singleton, of whom I had never heard but who turned out to live quite near. With his permission I should like to share with readers his views on *Seeing is Believing* which gave me the courage to pick up the pen once again. He wrote:

"Just a note of sincere thanks and appreciation for your wonderful little book Seeing is Believing. *I spotted it in Squire's Garden Centre at Shepperton and promptly bought two copies, one for a friend and one for my own library of bird books. I know photography can be a rather expensive pastime so I hope you get lots of customers because I am very much looking forward to future publications and we, your readers, should do all we can to encourage you to continue.*

I notice that you have published the book yourself and I salute you for your courage and enterprise in doing so – and making such a nice job of it too.

I particularly admire your comments on what used to be called 'fieldcraft' – painstaking observation and understanding of your subjects – and, above all, your appreciation of the imperative need to put the welfare of the birds above everything else. Unfortunately, not every so-called bird photographer these days shares your understanding of that need and the problem is undoubtedly worse than ever before now that superb photographic equipment and marvellous fast colour film are quite easily obtained. This has put temptation in the hands of many people who are more interested in winning 'wildlife photography' competitions or in selling bird pictures to agencies than in the welfare of the birds themselves.

You have obviously got all the qualities of a great naturalist and have completely mastered photo-technique in your chosen field. I am sure any further books you produce will be a great success.

Thanks again for an inspiring and beautiful book".

On reading Brian's letter I felt that I had reached my goal and even if I never sold another copy of *Seeing is Believing*, all the heartaches, the hours of laborious writing and correcting, the inevitable trail of rejection slips and, in the end, the sheer hard slog of "going it alone" were all worthwhile! Just as important too is the realisation that my "message" is getting through: get out and look around for yourselves at the wildlife we in Britain have been blessed with – do it now, please, before the ravages of pollution, climate change and habitat devastation destroy it all.

But this is a time, not for pessimism, rather for optimism that there are so many people in this country who do care deeply about our wild treasures. My hope is that this further little volume of my experiences with birds and other wildlife (more often than not in the company of Cliff Reddick, my good friend and fellow naturalist-photographer, whom many of you may remember from my earlier book) will stir more readers to discover for themselves the marvels all around us.

Derek Belsey, Shepperton.

Marvellous Montagu's Harriers

The birds we made our priority on the first trip to France were either the Marsh Harrier or Montagu's Harrier. After a lot of painstaking birdwatching over a three-day period Cliff found the nest of a Montagu's Harrier. It was in tall thick grass and well away from the beaten-track. A hide was introduced in the normal way but this time with many more precautions, for we knew Harriers could be very nervous.

With this in mind, every move was made with as little fuss as possible. We also draped grass and foliage over the hide so it would not be seen by anybody passing.

I had the first photo session – and it turned out to be one I shall never forget but for all the wrong reasons.

As Cliff left me it was agreed that we would each take turns for a two-hour spell in the hide. It was not long before the hen bird returned but I never heard her as she dropped to the side of the nest.

I sat motionless, not daring to breathe too loudly. She stood there looking magnificent as she checked that everything was in place before turning the eggs. Then a quick preen of her feathers, a last look around and she settled down to incubate her six eggs. The light was good for photography but I was very aware that the slightest noise could spook or even make her desert. I waited for a longer time than usual before attempting to take a picture. She now seemed relaxed so I closed my eyes and pressed the shutter button.

I slowly opened my eyes half expecting the bird to be gone but there she sat oblivious to the noise of my camera. Feeling more confident I took another six photographs as she pecked at loose pieces of grass that seemed to be annoying her.

I captured all the brooding shots that I wanted and now I waited for her to stand and turn the eggs. After about half an hour she obliged and my trigger finger was at the ready along with a spare roll of film. That's when it went all wrong as a gust of wind blew some of the grass we had draped over the hide across the lens of my camera.

There was nothing I could do as any movement from me would alarm her and I could not afford that at any cost. I looked at my watch and realised Cliff would not be back for another hour. All I could do was bite my lip and sit it out hoping the next session would make up for it. No way! For she did everything except cartwheels and headstands. I could not take a picture as frustration started to take a hold. As I've mentioned before, the picture is not always important but this situation was unreal as I was helpless to do anything.

The time seemed to drag but at last I could hear Cliff whistling in the distance, so did the Harrier and she flew off. I told Cliff what had happened but told him he could photograph with confidence and hopefully get the pictures I missed out on. This he did, but only after a long wait as I watched the bird return only to take off immediately. My first thought was that she had spooked but on a closer look through my binoculars I saw the reason and it was going to help my misfortune in the hide. The male Harrier had flown over the nest calling to his mate whilst carrying some sort of prey in his talons. He then flew skywards and started to circle as she flew up towards him. When she got to within ten feet of him she flipped onto her back whereon he dropped the food parcel which she caught in her talons. Then they both flew down to separate posts where she ate his offering as he looked on. As soon as she had finished he took to the air and made a couple of fly pasts over the nest with Cliff sitting in the hide wondering what had gone wrong. Then when the male thought everything was safe, he called her up from her post and escorted her towards the nest. He flew past and she dropped into the nest, obviously in the same way as when I occupied the hide.

Nothing like a good stretch.

All this had taken some time so I gave Cliff a bit longer in the hide before relieving him, plus it also gave the Harrier some breathing space.

Cliff, of course, got all the pictures that I didn't but I had seen my first-ever food-drop.

Cliff and I exchanged good and ill fortunes over a large filled baguette and a bottle of wine that evening.

We both had another session apiece in the hide where the Montagu Harrier gave us both some nice nest-side poses. I also saw another two food drops that week which was a bonus. I said to Cliff that I would like to do it all again but maybe another year.

"I held my breath."

A bird at ease.

A very bold Bluethroat

On the same trip to France another bird Cliff and I wanted to photograph was the Bluethroat. But after reading-up on the bird and how secretive it can be, we were not very confident. As I've mentioned before, birds, just like we humans, are individuals and the pair of Bluethroats we found on our very first day were going to prove the bird books wrong.

Both birds were flying about with beaks full of feed seemingly without a care in the world and it was not long before Cliff had located their nest in some undergrowth nearby. I then went off to photograph a pair of Avocets while Cliff prepared to make the first move with a hide onto the Bluethroats.

After about an hour I returned to find Cliff setting up his camera ready to photograph these supposedly secretive birds.

This pair were, as we put it, "bomb-proof" because all the time Cliff was moving the hide closer towards their nest they kept flying in with feed as though he did not exist.

Once Cliff was settled inside the hide I stood outside and gave him a running commentary as the birds approached the nest which gave him those extra seconds to be ready and focused up.

In no time at all Cliff had taken a roll of film. The evening was soon upon us and with the light fading we called it a day. Before we switched off the light at night two bottles of wine had washed down two rather large (Cliff-selection filled) baguettes while we talked about our first encounter with Bluethroats.

Over the next few days many hours were spent photographing or just watching this special pair of birds until we packed up the hide with our mission accomplished.

Well, not quite! For I returned a couple of days later to finish off a roll of film.

Without any cover at all I sat no further than six feet from the nest and still the Bluethroats perched up for me. Most of the time I forgot the camera and just sat and watched this special pair of unbelievable birds.

◀ Me camera shy? Maybe!
Me camera shy? No way!

A hungry brood.

Lookout Posts

I said I would like to try for Montagu's Harriers another year and here it is. After four days of rain, high winds and very few sightings of Harriers there was a short break in the weather. We soon found a nest but the hen bird seemed very nervous so we gave her a wide berth and concentrated on getting a photograph of the male Montagu's. It should have been easy but what was to follow will explain why it was not.

We watched his behaviour each time he fed his mate, which was to perch up on one of three posts. So it meant working a hide in to cover all of them with a camera.

This we did and I had first go in the hide to watch the Harrier's reaction. That's when "it should have been easy". The nightmare was about to unfold. The bird posted up and I had taken some two dozen photographs which were not going to be very good but it would give us a guideline. Unfortunately, the film in my camera had not moved on (no photographs) but there was worse to follow.

It was agreed that Cliff would have the next session the following day from closer range so after moving the hide we left.

After seeing Cliff into the hide in the afternoon I returned to our truck to watch the outcome from a distance. This is when I was confronted by a very irate French farmer whose arms and legs were waving all over the place as he ranted and raved at me. I, with very little knowledge of the French language, tried to explain that I was English, which was of no use. So I tried to humour him with phrases like "fermez la porte", "le crayon est rouge" and "avez vous du fromage", words that I thought one day might just get me out of the predicament I was now in! Not surprisingly it was to no avail and the upset farmer jumped into his little white van, driving off to remonstrate with Cliff.

From inside the hide Cliff had heard the commotion and decided it was time to explain everything, but the Frenchman would have none of it and carried on cursing with arms and legs still resembling a windmill. What he did not realise was that Cliff spoke fluent French so when he replied that we were not "English pigs", he stood back, obviously thinking he would be better off talking to me. But as much as Cliff tried, including offering to pay for any

The female landed first.

damage we may have caused (there wasn't any), the Frenchman would not calm down. His final words were, "if your hide is still there in the morning I will blast it with my shotgun". So much for the Common Market and the Channel Tunnel!

Once he had gone Cliff still wanted to chance it as the light was so good and we had already decided to leave for England the following day. I saw him into the hide for maybe the last time (who could tell?) and armed with my tripod I returned to our truck to keep a look-out. I saw the male Harrier return to one of the posts, just as our French farmer did. He was still waving his arms in the air so I did the same with my tripod whereon he returned to his van and drove off, still ranting and raving.

I did not know how Cliff was doing so I stayed but only to see our French friend return, this time with two other vans. I looked around and could see there was nowhere to run or hide so I stood my ground. There were plenty of fists being waved from inside the vans so I

▲ The male landed second.

◀ My trial run photograph.

waved back trying to look aggressive with my tripod. To my amazement (no, relief!) they drove-off which was my cue to rescue Cliff. He had heard the din and undone all the nuts and bolts that kept the hide frame together. As I lifted off the canvas cover Cliff was sitting with his camera gear packed-up as the four sides of the hide collapsed around him. There was no time for discussion as I bundled up the hide and we ran rather quickly to the safety of our truck. We drove back – also rather quickly – to our cottage with hardly a word spoken. Once safely back, many cups of tea were consumed as we relived the past couple of hours. Then, daring not to ask I said, "Cliff, did you by any chance get any photographs?". "Yes," he replied in a somewhat calmer manner. "I got both male and female Montagu's on the post plus a bonus shot of a Kestrel, but I never want to sit in a hide again waiting for both barrels of a shotgun to blast me and the hide into oblivion."

We both started to laugh as we knew the nightmare was over. As I mentioned before, birdwatching can be quite hectic at times.

Cliff landed this bonus shot of a kestrel.

Salt Pans to the Rescue

Although the main quarry on our rainy trip to France were birds of prey, it is always nice to have some back-up birdwatching and photography. This is where the salt pans usually come to our rescue. But because of the abnormal rainfall all the salt pans were flooded. After intensive searching I managed to find the only two that held nesting birds, a few Avocets and Black Winged Stilts, the only ones salt pans with ground or vegetation above water level. Most species of birds keep a low profile when it is raining so it was a welcome relief to sit in either of the hides to spend a little time birdwatching between and during showers. Both salt pans actually produced some great birdwatching, including several bonuses.

One such day from inside the hide on an Avocet; I watched Redshanks feuding and fighting with one pair copulating in front of the hide. Of course, by the time I got my camera into position it was all over and the only photograph I managed was of the cock bird running away in triumph. There was also a Black Winged Stilt acting funny to the right of me so I kept one eye on him. Sheld Duck kept dropping in to the left of me so I kept my other eye on them. A female Shoveller flew into some grass behind me but I could not watch her as I had run out of eyes.

Meanwhile the Stilt was now only ten feet from me and on a closer look I could just make out his mate sitting in a clump of grass. As I thought, a change-over was about to happen, what a bonus! I then slipped out of the back of the hide without any of the birds seeing me and met up with Cliff who had just done the same on the adjoining salt pan. He had a similar experience to me except the birds copulating in front of him were Avocets which he managed to photograph of course. On the way back to the truck we found the Shoveller sitting tight on eggs in the grass I had seen her fly into, which was another first for me. Many hours were spent in those two hides because of

▼ The Redshank ran away triumphantly.

"What is it Mum, a waltz or quickstep?".

the bad weather and a lot of good birdwatching was had.

Our last day had arrived so we went to pick up the hides early in case we bumped into our little French farmer. As we reached the hide on the Avocet she had not long hatched her first chick. Cliff said, “Quick, get your camera and try for a photograph”.

I just about managed to get into the back of the hide and set my camera up but the birds seemed nervous. I took only two photographs and left taking the hide with me. Once the truck was loaded we made a speedy retreat in case another nightmare was to unfold. I took one last look at the Avocets through my binoculars to see both Avocets at the nest with one little chick climbing aboard and to safety, which was the signal for us to reach the ferry back to England and also climb aboard to safety.

A very leggy Stilt.

“Here's looking at you babe.”

The early bird catches the Fish

Occasionally, during the winter months I'll have a wander about my local gravel pits, rivers and what little habitat that remains locally. In doing so I discover old nests that have been used the previous spring, which helps me to log what birds nested and where. This particular Saturday I went to watch a football match at Chertsey Town F.C. (a club I used to manage) and on the way home I decided on an hour's winter wander. First stop was at Chertsey Bridge, which stands on the River Thames, to check on a pair of Great Crested Grebes that nest in that area every year. This particular pair have nested quite early some years so I thought a quick look might be worthwhile.

Worthwhile? What an understatement! From the bridge I scanned the overhanging branches on the far bank of the small backwater where the Grebes usually build their nest. I could just make out one of the adult birds that seemed to be having an afternoon nap. That was until her mate appeared with a small fish in its beak. This seemed nothing unusual as they will often offer fish to their partner during courtship. But as he approached her a little grey head showed itself on its mother's back. I could not believe my eyes so I waited for it to happen again and sure enough within minutes Dad returned with another fish that was hastily gobbled up by the chick. I stayed and watched the Grebe family for the best part of an hour before leaving for home. There was a heavy frost that night and I thought the Grebe chick might not survive.

At 7 o'clock the following morning I was back at the river bank armed with my camera and tripod. To my relief both Grebes were there, but no sign of the chick. I managed to get onto the far bank for a closer look and to my relief I could just make out the top of a head above its mother's wing feathers. I managed to get a few photographs for the records before leaving for home once more but with a more confident feeling for the chick's survival.

On the Monday I 'phoned *Birdwatching* magazine and the B.T.O. to tell them about this early Great Crested Grebe chick. It turned out to be the earliest recorded Grebe that year although six other pairs had chicks in February.

But mine was born on February 12th and was still about when its parents reared a second brood, its brothers and sisters.

Which all goes to show that a wander in the winter is worthwhile.

◀ The early chick shows its head.

▲ The early chick twists its head.
◀ The family soak up the Winter sunshine.
▼ Dad arrives with more nesting material.

Ever decreasing Neighbours

Gradually all the wildlife habitat is disappearing in and around my village, none more so than an area that the Shepperton by-pass has cut through. It used to be mostly gravel pits, rough ground with a good mixture of wild flowers and weeds. Over the last thirty years I've watched many species of birds such as Kingfishers, Redshanks, Ring Plovers, Little Ringed Plovers (13 nesting pairs one year), Lapwings, Grey Partridges, Yellow Wagtails to name but a few. It also held one of the biggest Sand Martin colonies in Southern England. But they have all gone as all that's left is a small area of scrubland no more than 400 yards square by the side of a small gravel pit. Unbelievably some birds still manage to secure enough territory to nest successfully each year. Now I've heard that this remaining stronghold is going to be taken up for development of some kind.

▼ My first Sedge Warbler.

So this spring I decided to record and photograph as many birds as I could before all is lost. I sat for many hours watching the male birds as they arrived from their winter homes to claim a small territory and listened to them singing to attract a mate.

There seemed to be more species than there had been for the last couple of years so I concentrated on just four. Reed Warblers, Sedge Warblers, Whitethroats and Reed Buntings.

The Reed Warblers were no problem as I could tuck myself out of sight in the reed bed and without looking too hard had the choice of six nests to choose from. The Sedge Warblers were a different problem for I watched two males trying for the same female over several days and then they were gone. I thought it was possibly because the area was becoming too crowded and they had left for more space. Two mornings later everything fell into place. I was

▲ The ever alert cock Whitethroat.

▼ A Reed Bunting beauty.

watching two cock Reed Buntings fighting over three females when I saw the male Whitethroat drop into the undergrowth with feed. Then out flew the female who flew to a nearby bush and started preening. This was obviously a change over so now I had my Whitethroat I slowly walked backwards but still watching the spot that the male had dropped into when, almost by the side of my foot, the little Sedge Warbler flew out. After a quick look I found her nest with one egg at the base of some brambles. "Three down, one to go" as I moved further away only to catch a glimpse of one of the Reed Buntings with nesting materials. "What a morning," I thought to myself as I left for home and a hearty breakfast. I returned the following day to check that everything was in order. The Sedge Warbler had laid her second egg, the Whitethroat was still sitting on hers and there were now two Reed Buntings carrying nesting material. As I left for home and another breakfast, I thought there might just be some good birdwatching and photography over the next month.

The Reed Warblers that I had chosen duly obliged. The Sedge Warbler laid six eggs and reared five young. For the first three days they were very secretive when feeding their offspring. Both birds approached the back of the nest through the undergrowth and left the same way. But as the young got older the parents seemed to become oblivious to danger and flew direct to the nest in full view of a Sparrow Hawk that was often around. There was also a pair of Magpies snooping about so I placed extra brambles over and around the nest to deter them, and it worked.

The Whitethroats were going to be more difficult as they were more in the open so I had to camouflage my hide as not to attract the attention of local dog walkers and of people travelling along the by-pass. Again everything was successful and the Whitethroats also raised five young. I used the same hide on the Reed Bunting who had six young but the cock bird I had watched earlier had secured the services of all three females. This often happens and all he did between short breaks was to chase all three females throughout the day as they fed his off-spring in separate nests. I never did get a photograph of him but what I did get was all four species of birds that I had set out for.

I hope this remaining small pocket of habitat survives for a few more years as it's very special to me and extra special to our spring visitors:

The Reed Warblers
The Sedge Warblers
The Whitethroats
and The Reed Buntings

◀ A moth from mother Whitethroat.

Rewarding Reed Warblers. ▶

All's well that ends well

Each year this particular pair of swans return to their nesting site which is situated on a small backwater off the River Thames adjacent to the early nesting Great Crested Grebes on page 14 They built their new nest on top of last year's nest, which made it quite high.

Everything was going to plan as she laid six eggs but then, as in my first book about a pair of swans, there was torrential rain for two days. This time it was more dramatic for the river rose fast and, as high as the nest stood and with both swans trying to save it, they lost their eggs. The water level dropped and she laid two more eggs but the river rose once more and again the eggs were lost.

Undeterred, they built another makeshift nest further along the bank and away from the water's edge where she, unbelievably, laid another six eggs. Being concerned, I made regular visits to check on the swans and on each visit the pen seemed quite happy as she incubated her late clutch of eggs.

▼ The swan's final attempt.

The weeks passed and I started to worry about her as it seemed that she was on a fruitless mission. Then I got a 'phone call from a friend who was also checking on the swans. "Good news, she's hatched her first cygnet," he said. I don't know who was more relieved, me or the swans. The next day I paid them a visit hoping to photograph the swans and their new family.

My most distressing photograph. ▶

▼ "Would she make it this time?".

▲ My most satisfying photograph.

But another twist of fate greeted me for the cygnet had died just a few hours earlier. It was lying on the side of the nest next to its persevering mother. This was making me more uneasy about the situation so I 'phoned Dot Beason at the Egham Swan Sanctuary and explained the poor swans' plight.

Dot told me that this spring had raised many problems in the local swan population and it was just as well to leave the swan alone; she would leave the nest in her own good time. This she did eventually but she seemed very weak and her neck was sagging. Dot told me to keep an eye on her and if things did not improve she would take the swan in for a check-up.

Things did improve over the next few days and the last I saw of the swans was as they swam together downstream under Chertsey Bridge and out of sight.

I felt happy and sad at the same time as I thought of what they had been through.

They had built two nests, she laid fourteen eggs, eight of which she lost to the floods, hatched just one cygnet that lived for a few hours. All this spread over three months which makes it a real tale of complete disaster. But knowing this pair of swans as I do, I expect them to return next spring to try again.

I will certainly be there to help in any way to make sure they succeed.

Since writing this sad story another year has passed and my swans did return.

Was it going to be a repeat performance? As once again she lost her eggs through flooding but this time built a second nest on higher ground. Close by, nesting Coots and Moorhens hatched their young plus the early nesting Grebes were on their second brood. Another pair of swans locally were raising nine cygnets, but my swan was still sitting and I began to doubt whether she was going make it. But there was no need to worry, as Harry a friend of mine 'phoned to say the first cygnet had hatched. The following day I paid the swans a visit to find she and her mate were the proud parents of six cygnets.

As I sat and watched the happy family I had a feeling of relief and satisfaction as an old adage crossed my mind... *"If at first you don't succeed, try, try again"*.

Relaxing with Woodlarks and Stonechats

Because spring comes and goes so quickly, I try to cram in as much birdwatching as I can between April and July. It sometimes becomes a bit hectic so it is nice to venture further afield for a change. Every year Cliff and I make a visit to a little copse we know in Sussex to watch and hear the nightingales. It was a beautiful Saturday morning and on arriving at the copse the males were in full song. We sat in the truck for some time just listening before getting out to look. Every now and again one would show itself and then it was gone. We spent the best part of an hour looking and listening to what we think was maybe seven birds before deciding a breakfast should be the next thing on the agenda. So it was back in the truck and back to Surrey via a "Little Chef" where we demolished a full English breakfast and two pots of tea. Bellies full and batteries recharged our next quest was to find some Woodlarks and a pair of Stonechats that had eluded Cliff last year. After reaching our destination, a Christmas tree plantation near Shere in Surrey, we reached the stile just in time to see a Woodlark fly into some bracken with nesting material. We both put our thumbs up to one another before walking another fifty yards only to hear "Tsak Tsak", the harsh call of a male Stonechat that was perched up on a small piece of bramble. Cliff said, "Well that was hard work, both species in less than five minutes," and I replied "Don't knock it, how many times does it happen?"

Because it was one of Cliff's birdwatching areas he would work two hides in over the next few weeks.

He 'phoned me up in due course to tell me that "The hides are in place and ready for your

Very active Woodlarks. ▶

Lordship." I duly turned up with my camera gear and Cliff walked me into the Woodlarks' hide and leaving me hopefully to enjoy an easy photographic and birdwatching session. I was not to be disappointed as both Woodlarks and Stonechats were very obliging.

The Woodlarks' nest was built on the ground in some old bracken and gorse. I sat back and waited for either bird to return. It was not long before I heard a soft call as if to say, "We're on the way," and both birds walked slowly towards the nest where their young were waiting with open beaks. Every now and then one of the Woodlarks put its head deep into the nest and actually raised the young off the ground to clean up the nest. Each time they returned I was fascinated by the way they walked, it was almost like a waddle. Brilliant birdwatching, brilliant birds and, I forgot to mention, brilliant songsters.

It was now time for the Stonechats and making sure both birds were out of sight I quickly entered the hide. I had my camera set up in five minutes and had taken my first photograph in five and a half minutes. They were definitely another pair of "bomb-proof" birds and had also built their nest in some gorse and bracken. Before each visit to the nest they perched up on the piece of bramble where we had seen the cock bird previously. This was easier than the Woodlarks as they were back and forth all the time, mostly with bees as the main source of food. Occasionally one would bring a red moth that made the picture even more colourful.

It also seemed as if both birds were posing for me as they turned one way and then the other before dropping into the nest.

I packed up my camera gear and hurriedly left. Climbing the stile I looked back to thank both the Woodlarks and Stonechats for two hours of the most relaxing birdwatching one could ever have. Tomorrow I would be back to my hectic ways before spring passed me by.

▼ A beautiful female.

A handsome male. ▶

Feeding time for the Woodlarks.

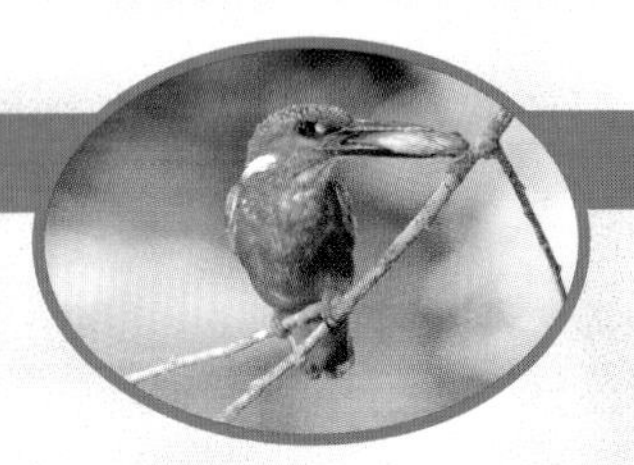

Remembering a Red Throated Diver

◀ A heart-thumping picture.

▲ A delightful Diver.

Cliff and I had been granted a licence to photograph a Red Throated Diver, but unfortunately not on the island where we were staying, for there had been little rainfall prior to our arrival on the Shetlands and water levels were low on most lochs.

This gave the Divers no suitable nesting sites and, as much as we searched, we could not find one.

But at the back of our cottage there was a pair nesting on a small loch. We informed the local licensing office and explained our predicament. They were very understanding and because no other licence was being used that week, gave us permission to erect a hide for photographing the Divers.

This we did at once, on the furthermost part of the loch, but on checking the nest, discovered that the birds had lost their egg, presumably to a Gull or Skua. While all this was happening it started to rain so we left the hide up and trudged back to our remote cottage to dry out and mull over the Divers and our bad luck.

The following morning we were up and off early as usual to move our other hides in on other nests but when passing the loch we could not believe our eyes, for the Diver was sitting again.

All was not lost as when we returned later she was off the nest and a quick look revealed another egg had been laid. It took many man hours and moves with the hide over the next few days to get it into a favourable and secure position but it was going to be worth it. It is very hard for me sometimes to put into words what I witness in birdwatching and I don't think I will ever get a more heart-thumping experience than the one with the Red Throated Divers. I was to have the first session in the hide. On our approach to the loch the sitting Diver slipped off the nest and swam some distance away. Once inside the hide and after Cliff had disappeared from the skyline, I heard one of the Divers call. I looked out to see the female swimming slowly back towards me.

This was one of the most exciting moments in all the years of my birdwatching. I had never seen a Red Throated Diver in the wild, let alone being 16 ft. from its nest.

I sat holding my breath as she left the water and clumsily climbed to the side of the nest before tidying it up and settling down on the eggs. I say eggs for she had now laid

Danger looms!

a second. She sat with her back facing me for the best part of an hour. It started to drizzle with rain and became overcast but I was not worried because this was another first for me.

What a first ! For she then stood up and turned the eggs before settling down again but this time side on to me. That was when my heart started thumping as I realised how beautifully marked this majestic bird was. I watched her preen herself and turn the eggs once more before Cliff showed himself on the far side of the loch. She laid flat and slowly slipped off the nest into the water to reappear yards away close to some lochside foliage. Cliff then took over and was lucky enough to photograph both birds at the nest.

We both had more time with the Divers the following day but it never compared with those first moments I shared with her and words can never describe them.

I did get one picture in the sunlight.

Waiting for the Wheatears

Each spring I wait for the Wheatears to arrive from their wintering grounds and stop off on my local farm to feed before continuing their journey northwards. Then, in late summer I wait for them again to return for a refill before flying back to their winter abodes.

Each time, I try unsuccessfully to get some long range photographs for record purposes, so when I knew that Cliff and I were off to the Shetlands, I felt more confident, for the islands are one of their breeding strongholds. But during our stay they only showed themselves occasionally. Cliff tried to assure me that they were on eggs. I doubted him a little until, two days before we were due to leave the Shetlands, Wheatears were everywhere, carrying feed. Every stone wall had a pair nesting and we became spoilt for choice, even though time was running out. We still had hides on the Arctic Skua, Whimbrel, Curlew, Oyster Catcher, the Gull colony and the Red Throated Diver. So we knocked up a frame with some old driftwood, draped an old tattered hide over it and tried to secure it the best we could with some heavy rocks. Because it was continually flapping about in the strong winds we were worried that it might spook the Wheatears. There was no need for they sometimes perched up on it before flying in to feed their young. The weather turned foul and it seemed our DIY carpentry was going to be a lost cause. This was the day I spent in the Red Throated Diver's hide when she sat with her back facing me. It was on my way back to our cottage still cursing my luck when it suddenly changed. There was a break in the clouds and the sun came out but looking skywards I could see it would not be for long. So I hurried towards the Wheatears' hide – still flapping in the wind – and set up my

The female with feed.

A small but lovely picture.

One of my favourite pictures.

camera. Both birds were flying in at regular intervals but I felt uncomfortable inside the hide for it was now in shreds and it was all I could do to hold it together with both feet and one hand while trying to photograph with my other. After about ten minutes the heavens opened up again and I hurriedly packed up my camera gear and ran to the cottage. As I took off my soaked clothing and knowing that I had taken just four photographs, I wondered whether it was all worth the effort. It was a pleasant surprise when my slides dropped through my letter box and, looking at the photographs of the Wheatears, I could see they were not half bad.

After a closer look I realised that waiting for the Wheatears was worthwhile after all.

Suddenly a Sentry Bird

I found photographing Oyster Catchers very similar to Lapwings. There is always a "sentry bird" which takes to the air in alarm when any sort of danger appears. That means it can spot you over a quarter of a mile away. A lot of patiencc is needed and keeping out of sight is essential.

I knew there was a pair nesting close to a colony of Black-headed Gulls that we had a hide on, so there was a good chance to watch the Oyster Catcher returning to its nest while

▼ The Oystercatcher settles down.

The centry bird raises the alarm.

photographing the Gulls. This I tried and at first it seemed a good idea until a Skua or Herring Gull or Lesser Black Backed Gull made an appearance. Then up went the Oyster Catcher sentry bird which alarmed both his mate and all the Black Headed Gulls. But eventually peace prevailed and I managed to get some very rewarding pictures. Now it was time to watch for the Oyster Catcher to return so I looked out the side of the hide to find it settled down on its nest – or so I thought. I focused her up in my camera but before I could take a photograph she got up and walked away! I could see no eggs but I could see Cliff in the distance walking towards me which explained everything.

I got out of the hide and had a closer look at where the bird had been sitting and, sure enough, there were no eggs. All the birds were in the air so I joined Cliff and we made a hurried departure so the birds could get back to their nests. The next day I saw Cliff into a hide we had on a Whimbrel before returning to watch the Oyster Catcher. I settled down in the hide to await its return but the wind had got up and it was all I could do to keep the hide from blowing away. All the Gulls returned almost immediately but there was no sign of the Oyster Catcher. With my feet astride and holding the hide cover firmly on the ground it wasn't exactly comfortable. I was about to give up when I heard the Oyster Catcher call and appear some 50 yards away to my left. Gradually she ventured towards me in a zig zag fashion and then sat down about 10 yards away as she did the previous day. It was then that I remembered the first Lapwing I photographed had done exactly the same. She made three more moves each time settling down on an imaginary nest before she called and walked to just 9 ft. from me.

I looked closer and could see the eggs in front of her and wondered if I was too

The drip was ready to drop.

One Mum and Chick.

Another Mum and Chick.

close. She moved the eggs about with her long beak before settling down seemingly content. The sun came out, the wind dropped, my camera was on the go and I was also content. After a while I stopped photographing to watch a little bead of water that ran from the top of her beak to the bottom before falling to the ground. Then another one formed and did the same thing and then another then zzzzzzzz! I awoke to the sound of the Gulls and Oyster Catchers taking to the air, Cliff was on his way towards me.

Sleeping Beauties

The Whimbrel asleep.

The Arctic Skuas' nest was not too far away from the Whimbrels' so we set up hides a fair distance away from one another. As we already had other hides in the vicinity we could make several moves on one trip. After a few days we were ready to make a final move on both birds but that night the wind and rain got up and on arriving at our hides in the morning we were to find them flattened. The Skuas' hide had been blown some fifty yards away, broken up and next to useless.

This caused Cliff to half blame me for not putting enough rocks in the pockets of the hide to keep it more secure. It was just as well, it helps to let off steam when you are getting continual upsets. After we had both calmed down, repairs were carried out on all the hides and roped down again before re-building the Skuas'.

By the end of our stay on the Shetlands we were ready to photograph both the Whimbrel and the Arctic Skua. Normally when photographing at the nest there is usually some sort of action, but these birds were an exception. The Whimbrel returned in no time at all, walking straight to the nest and settling down on the eggs without a pause. Within five minutes she dropped off to sleep occasionally opening one eye to look around. I told Cliff and he said, "If you think the Whimbrel's boring you wait until you photograph the Arctic Skua."

He was not far wrong except it did perform a couple of "dragging the wing" displays before approaching the nest. Then, like the Whimbrel, she walked straight to the nest and settled down on the eggs. Again within minutes she closed her eyes only to open them again to look to the right and to the left before nodding-off. I say nodding-off because in all the years of birdwatching I have never seen a bird drop off to sleep whilst incubating its eggs. This bird actually went to sleep and her head gradually fell backwards until it jolted upright before closing her eyes again.

I looked through the camera again just as the Skua's head jolted upright once more. I could not help chuckling to myself as I packed up my camera and tripod.

This story I've since told to many audiences when giving illustrated talks and they all find it amusing.

I guess the Arctic Skua is not as uninteresting as I first thought.

▲ The Whimbrel stirs.
▼ The Whimbrel awake!

◀ Zzzzzzz!

▼ "Me asleep?—never!"

A curious Curlew

I often wonder how birds sometimes define danger so when a particular Curlew showed me, it was another step towards understanding them. She had built a nest in a clump of heather only a few yards away from a small road that ran down to our bay.

When Cliff and I first noticed her she sat very tight and what small amount of traffic that passed she seemed to take in her stride. Thinking that this could be an easier bird to photograph than the other Curlews we had found, a hide was moved in over the next few days.

She was a very obliging bird except we never realised that birds can distinguish one vehicle from another. She must have had our green truck and the noise of its engine in her memory bank because for every vehicle that approached, including the postman's, she just lay quite flat in the nest until they had passed. But before our truck came into view she would get up from off her eggs and slowly walk away to a vantage point to watch the outcome. Once one of us was in the hide and the truck had moved off out of sight she would stand motionless for some time before calmly making her way back to the nest and, after turning the eggs, settling down.

▼ The Curlew approaches the nest.

The nest was cleverly built in a clump of heather and we knew if we could get the chicks hatching there was a very good chance of some exceptional photography. But the day they hatched it started to rain and the light was dull to say the least. Exceptional photography it wasn't but she and her chicks gave us birdwatching of the highest quality. Cliff and I both managed two sessions apiece without our truck so as not to disturb her too much.

During my second session I hardly took a photograph as I sat enthralled watching the Curlew chicks tumbling about the heather with Mum forever scolding and calling them back to the warmth and security of the nest.

It was a piece of birdwatching that I will always cherish and one I get a great deal of pleasure talking about, so much so that I made up a small poem about her:

Cars passed by day and night,
Still our Curlew sat very tight,
But out of sight she would tuck,
If ever she saw or heard our truck.

▲ "Come here—The truck's coming."

◀ "Stay here until it's gone."

▼ "The coast is clear—out you come."

Three hours with an Otter

Our Otter rolls in the seaweed.

It was our last morning on the Shetlands and we had just one remaining hide to pick up on the way to catch the ferry home. It was on an Oyster Catcher about to hatch, something I was looking forward to. I stepped out of our cottage for a last look around only to catch sight of an Otter feeding inshore not more than twenty yards out. I called to Cliff who immediately said, "I'll go and get my camera," which I knew would be fatal. After a short discussion it was agreed that there would be many other opportunities to photograph an Oyster Catcher, but an Otter? A plan of approach was hastily worked out. Cliff would gradually work his way along the cliff top to my hand signals. That meant every time the Otter dived he would have to make ground towards a vantage point where he might possibly get a photograph, if lucky.

After several dives by the Otter and the same number of scrambles by Cliff, plus waiting for the Otter to finish eating its catch, the Otter came out of the water, up onto some rocks to preen its coat and rest.

Unfortunately, that was some 50 yards along the shore from where Cliff was lying. We both had to keep low so as not to be seen or to let it get our scent. This all took valuable time and I started thinking about the Oyster Catcher I could be photographing. Eventually the Otter returned to the water to carry on hunting for eels that seemed to be its main food. Once more I started my "tic tac" hand signals and once more Cliff started his scrambling along the cliff top. Between the Otter's dives I watched it catch and eat ten small eels before once again coming out of the water, this time not too far from where Cliff was positioned. Slowly but surely I managed to direct Cliff to a favourable spot to photograph from. He poked his camera over the top of the cliff and just for a moment it seemed that the Otter had seen it, so I signalled to him to stay still.

It worked and once the Otter turned its head the other way, I urged Cliff to make his final move up to his camera. He was now over a hundred yards away from me and although I could not hear his camera clicking I knew he was getting our pictures by his thumbs up signal. I say 'our' pictures because without a team effort at times, situations are impossible. Once Cliff had finished his photography he moved backwards on his stomach and out of sight.

Back at the cottage we both agreed the effort had been worthwhile. It had taken three solid hours of patient Otter stalking – not too far divorced from certain birdwatching experiences.

We packed the last few things onto the truck before moving off to pick up the hide from off the Oyster Catcher. She had just hatched out her fourth chick and, as much as I would have liked to photograph and watch for a while, there was no time so I had to be content with the thought that at least I saw everything that the Otter had done while Cliff was crawling about, and as we drove towards the ferry we both realised how privileged we had been to share those three hours with the Otter.

A not so Common Sandpiper

On the very first day of our second trip to Wales, Cliff found the nest of a Common Sandpiper that we had previously missed. The hen bird was sitting on four eggs in a field full of grazing cows.

A hide was immediately erected some distance away from the nest ready for what turned out to be a very eventful next few days.

The cows seemed to congregate in the area of the nest so the Sandpipers were forever in danger of getting their eggs trampled on.

Action had to be taken and, after gaining permission from the local farmer, we nailed up a strand of barbed wire around the area to safeguard both nest and eggs.

With the hide now in position many pleasing photographs were taken over the next few days.

But then it all went wrong!

I had walked Cliff into the hide and left with his dog, Tarka, for a casual stroll only to have one of

The Sandpiper is well hidden.

◀ "Peek-a-Boo."

▲ The cows were never far away.

the heifers break away from the herd to chase her.

Cliff was obviously unaware of the situation and was sitting contentedly in the safety of the hide waiting for the returning Sandpiper. Meanwhile, the heifer chased Tarka across a nearby river, then upstream and downstream before giving up the chase and returning to the herd.

It took some time to calm Tarka but eventually, after seeing the herd in the far distance, she came to my side and we continued our stroll toward a little copse where I sat and watched a pair of Redstarts feeding their young away from the nest.

Both Tarka and I were now more relaxed, which was handy as it was time to relieve Cliff from the hide. On approaching the hide it became obvious that Cliff was having trouble of his own.

Two calves had managed to get under the barbed wire and were standing too close to the Sandpipers' nest for comfort. Cliff, inside the hide, was helpless as one of the calves was only inches from the eggs and the slightest scare could cause it to trample on them.

Cliff, with fingers crossed, sat patiently until the calf had moved away from the eggs before jumping out of the hide with his arms and legs waving about like a lunatic.

But his ploy worked as both nest and eggs were still intact.

Once Cliff had calmed down we decided a further strand of barbed wire was needed and within half an hour this was done. As we walked away we stopped to look back and watch the Sandpiper returning apprehensively to its clutch of eggs, hopefully to spend the rest of the day in peace.

We continued on our way, discussing how my five-mile run with Tarka, a roll of barbed wire, hammer and nails, and a now sedate Clifford, had saved another nest and eggs.

This was a case of where it was right to interfere with nature.

Manoeuvres with Whinchats

A third short trip to Wales for a few days in May was agreed on. Cliff booked into a B&B on the Friday, a small place where we had stayed before, and I joined him on the following Monday.

Cliff (bless him) had spent two days in pouring rain but had still managed to get hides onto a Redstart, a Wood Warbler and a bird he has been trying for for some years, a Whinchat. As I arrived, the weather cleared for a few hours which gave Cliff a chance with the Redstart as I followed his directions to the Whinchats' nest.

Once settled down inside the hide I waited in anticipation for the Whinchats to show themselves. Within minutes the female perched up on a nearby thistle with a beak full of feed. She sat for a while before dropping down to the nest to feed her young and back on the thistle for a quick look about, then off in search of more food.

The cock bird was not long behind her and carried out the same procedure. I sat back and watched for the first few visits without taking a photograph, which I was about to regret. For over the brow of the hill appeared an army helicopter that hovered above me. I looked out from the hide and could see a soldier looking down at me through a pair of binoculars and I was pretty sure he wasn't birdwatching. After a few circles above me the helicopter flew off and I settled down again. But not for long as the next I knew was an army jeep pulling up beside my parked car. Two soldiers got out and started to look it over, whereby I left the hide to show myself to them. They asked me if it was my car and what I was doing on army property. After I explained, showed them some sort of identification and told them about the Whinchats, they wished me all the best in my pursuits before driving off.

Back to the hide once more where a roll of film was quickly taken in case I became the target of an all-out attack! With my camera geared up I left the Whinchats to carry out their parental duties in peace.

When I told Cliff, he laughed but said "Don't worry, there will be plenty of time to get another session in."

Don't worry! Down came the rain for the next 24 hours. But our patience was rewarded as the sun showed itself once more and it was off to the Whinchats for another go.

Once back inside the hide I sat and waited, again not for long as both birds appeared, seemingly at peace with the world. But then they started scolding and flying in all directions. I thought to myself, "Not again!

◀ A magnificent male.

A Stunning female. ▶

What could it be this time?". I looked about but could see no one else. Then I wondered if the birds were trying to encourage their young to leave the nest, or could the young have actually already left the nest? It might be anything and, as I've said before, the birds are more important than any photograph, so it was time to leave and watch from a safe distance. As I opened the back of the hide all was explained, for up on a telegraph pole was a Buzzard which, on seeing me, flew off. At once the birds stopped scolding and started to bring food to their young who were still in the nest. Hence an hour of brilliant birdwatching and photography in beautiful evening light.

On driving back to our B&B I had a slight chuckle to myself as I realised that on both sessions at the hide I had been interrupted by two species of birds – one Buzzard and one helicopter.

It turned out to be my last chuckle as down came the rain for the next two days.

But that's all part of birdwatching.

His wings resembled the helicopter's. ▷

▽ A shaft of sunlight catches the male Redstart.

One lost Little Grebe

For the past two years the Little Grebes that once nested on the pond by my local farm had not shown themselves. So I was pleased to hear them calling on a nearby gravel pit this year. After a thorough search I found them nesting just five feet. from the bank and seeing a photo opportunity not to be missed, I worked in a hide ready for the action.

The female had six eggs and all was running smoothly until work on an adjoining pit caused a 12-inch rise in the water level. Both birds frantically gathered weed to build-up their nest, while I had to secure my hide (which was nearly afloat) and sit on a milk crate wearing a pair of wellingtons.

The Grebes seemed oblivious of my presence as they dived below the water for nesting

▼ A comfort zone for one.

▲ A comfort zone for two.

material before emerging with a "plop". That was, until one of them made a louder "plop" as it appeared inside the hide between my wellingtons. I don't know who was the more surprised.

Nevertheless, they carried on with the nest renovations and only one egg was lost, which pleased me. But what did not please me was missing the chicks hatching. So, knowing that the Grebes sometimes use the nest as a resting platform, I entered the hide and waited. It was not long before one of the birds returned and four chicks tumbled from its back onto the nest. The mate continually brought food back to them until climbing on the nest itself, a fifth, dead chick fell from its back. It had not survived and I couldn't help wondering how long the chick had been dead on its parent's back. Both adult birds continued feeding the other four chicks, seemingly ignoring the dead one. I couldn't ignore it so when the little Grebe family had finished their rest and swam off, I got out of the hide and removed it.

The next and final visit I made was more happier as I could see the whole Grebe family feeding together. So I gathered up my hide and left for home to write this little story on Little Grebes.

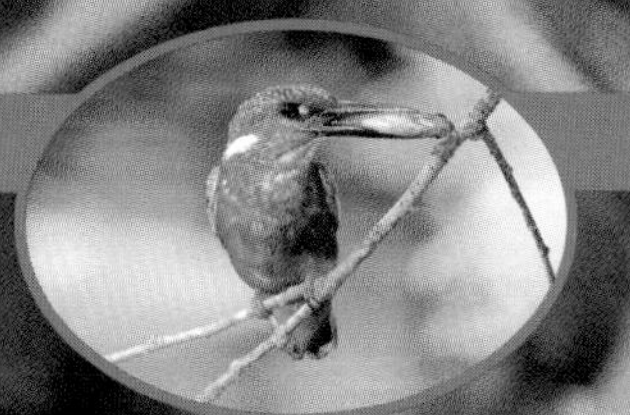

Memories

▲ A feather for a feathered friend.

▲ This Robin took over Tony's greenhouse.

◀ Ring-necked Parakeets took over this apple tree.

▼ This Jay took its share of apples.

A puffed out Puffin climbs the hill.

A glorious Guillemot.

"A wonderful Waxwing."

"To-woo are you looking at?"

For the love of Lapwings

With the decline in most of our British birds it's nice to be able to watch Lapwings each year on our local Laleham farm. I always make sure of spending some time to watch their aerobatic displays above the fields before they land and show an orange rump below their tail feathers to attract a mate. I've always had a soft spot for the Lapwing, possibly because it was one of the first birds I tried to photograph and, may I add, with a lot of difficulty. This year was no exception so I put a hide up early knowing how spooky Lapwings are.

With the help of Charles Bransden (farmer), his staff and Mercer (the local bird ringer) we managed to locate over 35 Lapwing nests and eggs on the farm. Unfortunately, being a ground-nesting bird they are vulnerable to marauding Crows and a local fox who seems to know exactly when the Lapwings are at their nesting peak. Last year, over a period of several nights, Reynard raided most of the nests but the Lapwings that lost their eggs laid a second clutch and, although the fox again took his quota, many chicks were hatched successfully. As I've mentioned before, Lapwings are ever alert to danger so when it appears a sentry bird takes flight with an alarm call and all the nearby nesting birds take to the air before returning to their nests when they think it's safe to do so. This makes photography very frustrating but, with a little patience, I managed to capture on film the very first Lapwing chicks being hatched on the farm this year.

Once the chicks were dry, I watched them being led away by both parents to the safety of the dense undergrowth that is left purposely by the farmer.

By the end of June, Mercer had recorded and ringed 69 Lapwing

One contented Lapwing.

chicks. Some were taken by the resident Crows but, as I walked about the farm it was very rewarding to see our combined efforts resulting in fully fledged Lapwings making their first solo flight.

Next year I'll be waiting once again to watch our Laleham Lapwings performing their aerobatic displays in the shadows of the ever-passing jumbo jets in and out of Heathrow airport.

For the love of Lapwings, long may the Lapwings of Laleham farm survive.

◀ She swallows the evidence.

▼ Two contented Lapwings.

Surprising Sparrowhawk

The Lapwings on Laleham farm have their enemies such as Crows and the fox. But the farm's smaller birds have theirs in the shape of Magpies and a pair of Sparrowhawks.

One day, while checking out a bank where a pair of Kingfishers nest each year, I was surprised by a Sparrowhawk that flew low above my head and swooped up into a nearby willow tree. I was sure it was carrying a small twig or branch. So I sat out of sight and waited. Sure enough the female returned with more nesting material but flew off.

I took a quick look up into the willow tree and, as I thought, the hawk had taken over an old Crows' nest that I knew of. I gave the tree a wide berth for the next few weeks, as did the Kingfishers that usually nest in the bank beneath it. Although the nest was some 35ft. above the ground, by climbing up the bank next to it I could actually see into the nest, that was providing I could cut my way through about 15ft. of dense brambles and pile up six pallet boards with a hide on top! This I did over a period of days but making sure not to disturb the Sparrowhawk. I left a strip of brambles in front of the hide, with just enough room to poke my camera through, a ruse which worked very well.

She laid four eggs and hatched four chicks but lost one early.

I spent many hours in the hide watching the Sparrowhawks raising their family without taking too many photographs because the light was never very good. The male brought back to the nest many species of prey but mainly Blue Tits and Great Tits. One bird I'm sure was a Linnet because the previous year I saw the male take one from off the top of a cabbage. I had a hide by the side of that particular cabbage as in its leaves was a beautiful nest with six eggs, minus one Linnet. That unfortunate little bird helped to feed last year's Sparrowhawk chicks, but that's nature for you.

This pair of hawks were different to the previous pair I had photographed as this male brought the prey to the nest and had a quick look at his offspring before flying off. The other male I had pictured, used to call his mate

▼ The hen bird spreads her feathers.

A very attentive Mother.

Both birds at the nest—very unusual.

off the nest and passed the prey to her before flying off to hunt for more. Very, very seldom did he come to the nest, which goes to show how some birds differ in their ways.

I tried to pay a visit as often as I could to this year's Sparrowhawk family because I would never get a better chance to study their behaviour. I watched many feeding sessions and many visits to the nest by the male. But they were very brief as the female became very aggressive if he outstayed his welcome.

I allowed Mercer to ring the chicks for future records before I had my last few visits to the hide.

I'm sure the young hawks had got to know me because the day I dismantled the hide they were on various branches in the tree. Once I had everything packed away I returned to the nest for one last look and to thank the birds for a month of fantastic birdwatching. I was amazed to see all three chicks standing to attention on the nest and, if I could understand bird talk, I'm sure they were thanking me! As I drove away the female Sparrowhawk flew over my car and called.

Was she also saying, "Thank you," or maybe, "See you next year?".

I hope so, for I will return next year and if the hawks do the same I will write Chapter Two.

If they don't, I shall watch out for a flash of turquoise blue and the Kingfishers to take up residence again.

I'm sure they were saying "Goodbye".

Capers with a Kentish Plover

An unforgettable female.

Garry's father had given us the use of his holiday apartment in Portugal. We took up his generous offer, "we" including my wife Pat, the most important person not to be acknowledged in my first book *Seeing is Believing* (my ear has been bent ever since!).

I managed to sneak a hide into our baggage just in case there might be any birds to be photographed.

Birds to be photographed?

Just for starters we found five Little Owl nests, Sardinian Warblers, Fantail Warblers plus, on one salt pan, no fewer than 17 Avocets, with Little Terns and Black Winged Stilts everywhere. Also there seemed to be Kentish Plovers nesting on

▲ A marvellous male.

every spare piece of shingle. There was so much happening I could have written a small book about it!

For instance:

a Little Tern tried to take over a Black Winged Stilt's nest with three eggs by laying one of its own. This resulted in many skirmishes at the nest, which the Stilt eventually won.

and:

a Kentish Plover laid, and lost, three eggs in the middle of a shingle path but then laid another three a few yards away which she

This bird led us a merry dance. ▷

> happily incubated. (I recall a Little Ringed Plover doing the same thing back home in England.)

and again:

> on another day Garry and I approached one of the other Kentish Plover nests only to discover she had hatched out her three young.

Over the years I have seen the "injured wing display" by our own Little Ringed and Ringed Plovers as they try to lure you away from their chicks. But this particular Kentish Plover put on an academy award performance.

It started by dragging its wing along the ground towards us before turning away and falling some six feet into the shallow water of the salt pan. It then flipped on to its back somehow and proceeded to flutter in the water as though it were drowning. But in no time at all it had reached dry land, a good hundred yards away from where it had started, taking with it two mesmerised birdwatchers. The Plover then took to the air in a large circle before returning to the safety of its mate and chicks.

The last example of bird "happenings" was of me trying to photograph one of these fascinating little waders.

The pair I chose were some distance away from all the other nesting birds so less disturbance would be caused, I thought. What a mistake!

Five moves were made with my hide leaving just one more before the camera could start clicking.

Each time I noticed it was the cock bird that returned to the nest. We made the last move with the hide in the cool of the morning about seven o'clock, but as I lifted up the flap out slid a snake of some 3ft. How Garry and I avoided falling back into the water I shall never know as we made a quick retreat.

After we thought the snake would be miles away I approached the hide with a little apprehension and a large forked stick. A more than thorough search was made before I sat down to photograph, with my tripod and camera still slightly shaking.

△ An egg mix up.

The cock bird returned to the nest within minutes and settled down on its eggs as my camera worked overtime. I sat back and waited for a change-over at the nest so I could photograph the hen bird. I heard her call on her return and he duly left the nest before she appeared nervously.

I managed to get a few photographs but she did not seem at ease with the hide and flew off. Seeing that I felt the same about the snake I quickly removed the hide and left, still armed with my forked stick.

When I reached Garry he said he had watched both birds return to the nest which made me feel a lot easier. Then I replied, "Snakes alive, what a caper."

More Memories

A pair of friendly Fulmers.

▲ Cliffs' dog Tarka was a great companion.

◀ So was our dog Freda.

"Mum, are you sure we're sheep?". ▲

▲ "What are you doing Cliff?"

◀ "I've got him under control.

▼ "Well I did have", said Michael.

Mum returns with a meal.

"Forever amber."

I wish I hadn't left the nest.

"Well I did tell you not to."

▲ "What are you saying, mum?".

▼ A Great Skua shows its wings.

▲ Hungry mouths must be fed.

Another male Redstart. ▼

Acknowledgements

To all my generous sponsors:

Cliff Reddick for co-starring so admirably in this book.

John Penfold for his help and encouragement.

Charles Bransden and staff for their efforts to preserve nesting birds on the farm.

Nick Payne for his kind donation.

To everyone who bought my first book and those who buy this one.

Finally to Brian Singleton for all the text setting and his wonderful letter that prompted me to undertake the publication of this book.